Great Grapes
Grow the Best Ever

Annie Proulx

CONTENTS

Introduction

For most growers, the triumph of harvesting fragrant clusters of dusky-bloomed grapes in rose, blue-black, amber, purple, or light red bunches is its own reward — a test of gardening skill. Grapes are among the most desirable and best known fruits on earth, prized for their beauty, their place in classical legend and mythology, their succulence and varied flavors as luxury table fruits, their noble metamorphosis into wine, and their more utilitarian roles as sources of fresh juice and tasty jellies.

Grapes are a labor-intensive specialty crop, best grown by a patient, careful gardener with a feeling for the vine. Properly grown and ripened grapes are always in demand and bring good prices in the market and at roadside stands. This is one area where commercial growers cannot compete with the dedicated, small vineyard tiller who can best give the vines the attention they need to produce high yields of quality fruit. Growing grapes is a good way to augment your regular income, as well as stock a wine cellar and the pantry shelves — if you have the proper site and an inclination for this vine.

This bulletin will tell you how to grow grapes — from planting to harvesting.

Who Can Grow Grapes?

Grapes have the reputation of being fragile and difficult to grow. Many northern gardeners, convinced that all grapes are too tender for their fierce winters and uneven spring temperatures, do not even consider trying to grow them, yet some vines will flourish in regions of every state and in several Canadian provinces. Since 1843 when Ephraim Bull of Concord, Massachusetts, finally succeeded in breeding the native grape he named for his town, after more than 20,000 tries, grape breeders, and hybridizers have developed literally thousands of different grape varieties suited to an amazing range of climates and soils. A good rule of thumb is that if wild grapes grow in your area, you can grow plump and tasty domestic grapes of some kind.

Even in New England, successful commercial and amateur vineyards are proliferating. Several winemakers in the best southern New England sites are actually growing *Vitis vinifera*, the prima donna European wine grapes — a gardening feat once believed impossible in this region. Hardier cultivars (*cultivated varieties*), such as the Beta and Blue Jay will grow in the northern states and southern Canada, bred to withstand winter temperatures that plunge to 30°F below zero! Really determined vine growers can coax even the most delicate vines to fruition in a hothouse. In an especially sheltered, sunny, well-drained site — an optimum microclimate — you may be able to grow cultivars beyond their normal range. Northern grape growers have worked out wine growing, or viticultural, practices that protect and encourage their vines despite frost and snow. In the South Atlantic and Gulf states, Muscadine grapes will succeed where other cultivars cannot.

You can grow grapes successfully if:

- You choose the most suitable cultivars for your area, grapes that will ripen before killing frosts get them, or that will withstand hot, humid summers.
- You plant them in the most sunny, sheltered, well-drained place possible.
- You learn — and practice — every special growing technique that will give you and your grapes the edge over climatic vagaries.
- Don't give up if one variety fails to flourish. Only trial and error will enable you to match the best cultivar to your vinery.

The Best Climate

The best grape climates are regions where the growing season is 150 to 180 days, where relative humidity is low, and where summer rains are sparse rather than frequent. A week of cloud and rain in the final week of ripening may result in extensive crop losses.

Grape Yields

- 10 Concord vines grown 8 to 10 feet apart will yield about 50 quarts of juice a year.
- Each vine of bunch grapes will give between 5 and 15 pounds of fruit every season.
- One to two bushels of grapes yields enough juice to fill a 5-gallon carboy.

Grape growing will be difficult or impossible in arid desert regions without irrigation, in places with extremely short growing seasons, or with very severe winter temperatures.

Something to Think About

You should have a good idea of what you will do with your grape crop before your vineyard gets off paper. A quarter-acre of vines — about 100 plants — can give you a ton of fruit at harvest time. A ton of grapes fills 50 to 60 bushel baskets. Depending on the grape cultivar, this means up to 200 gallons of juice or wine.

If you are thinking of growing grapes commercially, even on a small scale, you should know that the costs of establishing a vineyard (posts, wire, vines, pesticide sprays, and hired labor) are estimated at about $4,500 an acre. The major cost is in the hired labor. Cultivation, vine training, pruning, pest control must all be done *when the vines need it*, or the crop may fail. The home grower who can attend to his or her vines without hiring paid help is way ahead of the game. Remember, too, that it takes three to four years before the vines will produce a crop.

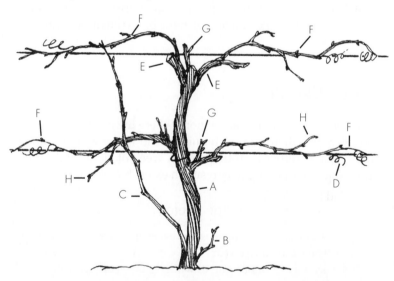

The major parts of a grapevine consist of the trunk (A), suckers (B), young replacement trunk (C), tendril (D), arm (E), cane (F), spur (G), and shoot (H).

Grape Growers' Vocabulary

Arms: The favored canes left on the vine after the rivals are pruned off. These arms produce fruiting shoots and canes for next year. After a season's production they are usually pruned off during the next dormant season and replaced.

Canes: The mature shoots late in the season. The word also means the year-old dormant wood of the preceding season. Most canes are pruned out during the dormant period before the new growth begins in the spring.

Cordon: *See* Trunk.

Cultivar: A cultured variety of plant especially developed for commercial or domestic cultivation. Cultivar is just a short form of cultivated variety.

Renewal canes: *See* Spurs.

Shoots: The young, succulent growth of the present season. Shoots grow from last season's buds and send out leaves, flowers, and fruit. When mature, they become the fruiting canes of the next season.

Spurs: Short, one- or two-bud canes deliberately left on the vine to become the arms and canes of the future.

Stripping: The process of removing all new growth in the event of frost damage.

Trellis: A number of wires strung on posts to support the fruiting arms of the vine.

Trunk: The main stock of the plant, also called the cordon. Some tender varieties may have two, or even three, trunks.

Basic Grape Types

There are basically three types of grapes: native wild grapes, *Vitis vinifera*, and hybrids.

The twenty-four to thirty species of wild grapes native to the United States comprise more than half of the world's species. The most familiar is the Fox Grape (*Vitis labrusca*) from which the Concord with its characteristic "foxy" taste was developed, the Riverbank grape, the Frost Grape, and the Muscadine Grapes of the South, of which the yellow-green, plum-flavored Scuppernong is best known. Some of the wild grapes are still gathered and used for jelly. The best have been hybridized by grape breeders in their search for hardy, disease-free, delicious fruits.

In the late nineteenth century vines were sent from the United States to Europe that carried *phylloxera*, a burrowing plant louse that feeds on grapevine roots. Although the American vines were resistant to phylloxera, the European wine grapes were not, and great and noble vineyards were devastated, especially in France. Today European vineyards are planted with *Vitis vinifera* grafted on native American rootstocks which are by nature resistant to phylloxera.

Vitis vinifera are the famous grapes of Europe from which the great wines come; and Riesling, Cabernet Sauvignon, Chardonnay, Pinot, and many others are the grapes that have made wine history. From their Mediterranean homelands, *Vitis vinifera* have been transplanted all over the world from South Africa to Russia. In the United States they grow especially well in California, Oregon, and Washington; but they are being successfully harvested and pressed elsewhere, even in New England. Some of the familiar dried raisins come from *Vitis vinifera*, but this crop is almost exclusive to California since it calls for a very long sunny season for the berries to develop the necessary amount of sugar.

There are also complex crosses involving *Vitis vinifera*, native American grapes, and the resulting hybrids themselves. Decades of intensive hybridizing by grape breeders have given commercial and home grape-growers many cultivars suited to nearly every climate from the cold north to the hot, humid Gulf Coast, and to a wide range of soils, from acid to fairly alkaline. These "bunch grapes," as they are often called, are used for table fruit, wine, fresh and canned juice, jellies, and cooking. They are the mainstay of the home grape-grower.

Many of the French hybrids carry the names of their breeders, as Georges Couderc, Seyve-Villard, who specialized in hybrid vines for warm climates; Baco, whose hybrids are important in the New York wine industry; and Seibel, who developed hundreds of specialized vines. Usually a number is attached to the name. For example, Seibel 13053 is a very early, hardy blue grape also known as Cascade. There are also American and Canadian hybrids, usually bearing simple place names, such as Niagara, Buffalo, Seneca, and the Canada Muscat. The Experimental Station in Geneva, New York, is one of the major American centers for grape hybridization. The Geneva-based New York State Fruit Testing Cooperative Association (NYSFTCA) annually offers its members promising new varieties of dessert and wine grapes developed at the Geneva station and elsewhere for home trial and testing.

The bunch grape hybrids are popular and extensively grown. They are easy to work with, bear early and regularly, and, like other grapes, are long lived, with a span of fifty years. Some cultivars are best for eating fresh, such as Seneca; others, like the Concord, are used in juice and jelly; some, like Foch and Seibel 9549 (De Chaunac) make very good wines.

Grapes Are Natural Swingers

Back in 1909, T. V. Munson, a man who knew a lot about grapes, wrote this advice "Grapes in trees are little bothered by rot and mildew. It is when the vines are held down on trellis near the ground in dense mass that these diseases attack the worst."

That, in a nutshell (or a grape skin), has been my observation, too. And I came to the conclusion a long time ago that one of the most important, if not *the* most important thing in growing good grapes, is good air circulation.

Not every gardener has the perfect spot to grow everything under ideal conditions, and sometimes must make do with what he has. The only place I have for growing grapes is around my garden fence, which runs north and south. Fortunately there is a high terrace just outside the fence and the air circulation is good.

Even so the white grapes, which tended to bear heavily, were one year infected with brown rot, and all the grapes along the fences were a loss. But one eager branch escaped upward and grew into a big hackberry tree just outside the fence. It was totally unaffected by the humid conditions that ruined the others; the big clusters of white grapes high up in the tree were beautiful to behold, even though I had to harvest them with a ladder.

Grapes, like strawberries, can be grown in almost every section of our country if we are careful to choose adaptable varieties. They come in a wide range of flavors, can be used for juice and jelly, and the trellises and arbors on which they are grown can be most attractive parts of our gardens or home grounds, creating pleasant shaded areas that are useful in landscape planning and for screening off undesirable view.

Louise Riotte, *The Complete Guide to Growing Berries and Grapes*,
Garden Way Publishing.

Planning Your Vineyard

Choose the Right Cultivars

The USDA has developed maps outlining four basic grape regions: the early-ripening grape area; the midseason ripening area; the late-ripening area; and the unique Florida and Gulf Coast area. These regional maps are a good general guide for selecting grape varieties to grow. In addition you should talk to your extension agent and, if possible, other grape-growers in your neighborhood. There is no substitute for experience in the vineyard.

If you intend to grow grapes commercially, even on a small scale, you will want to stick with dependable, safe cultivars that will not fail you at harvest time. If you are more adventurous, growing only for your own use, and if you don't mind an occasional crop failure, experiment with cultivars a bit beyond your range and join the NYSFTCA to try the latest from the fruit breeders' laboratories. Check the table in the back of this bulletin for varieties suited to your area and consult your local county agricultural agent or extension service for advice.

Choosing the Best Site

Choosing the right place for a vineyard is always important; for a northern gardener, it is a crucial decision. You may not be aware of it, but your land forms miniclimates of its own. Northern slopes are colder and receive fewer hours of sunlight.

Northern growers usually seek southeastern, southwestern, or southern exposures on long, gentle slopes with *good air drainage* — where the frost will roll down past the vines and settle in the flat lands and the valleys. Spring frosts probably cause more harvest losses than cold winters because a late frost at flowering time can severely damage the season's crop of grapes. Although planting on a northern slope leads to late flowering, which in turn reduces the risk of frost harm, such slopes lose too many hours of precious sunlight so vital to the fruit's maturation and ripening process.

Most vineyards lie on slopes. Vineyards on northern or southern slopes with rows running east and west, not only hold the soil in place, they take advantage of the prevailing westerly winds that quickly dry and aerate the grape foliage, reducing the chances of disease. Grapes are extremely sensitive to dampness. Hot, humid conditions, as in parts of the South, are conducive to numerous diseases and fungi that attack grapes.

Some of the most favorable sites for vineyards are south or east or southeast of large lakes. Temperature changes in spring and autumn are slow and moderate in these locations, with less chance of untimely frosts. Winds off the lake keep the grape foliage dry and healthy.

Be as deliberate in placing your vineyard as you would an orchard; grapevines live and bear for more than fifty years.

The Soil

There is a winegrower's saying in Burgundy: "If our soil weren't the richest in the world, it would be the poorest." The classic European wine grapes are largely grown in chalky, sandy, or shale soils where nothing else will thrive. Such soils encourage the plant to put its energy into the fruit rather than foliage. Although these famous, "noble" soils are poor in some nutrients, they are rich in the mineral elements which contribute markedly to the final flavor and aroma of the great wines.

Fortunately for grape lovers elsewhere, the vine will grow in many different soil types. Well-drained, deep, fertile loams are excellent, yet grapes will thrive on soils containing clay, slate, gravel, shale, and sand. Gravelly, stony soils generally drain well, and they absorb and reflect the sun's warmth to give the vine bottom heat.

Very dry and very wet soils are bad for grapes. A soil that drains poorly is quite unsuitable, as are shallow soils underlaid by hardpan, gravel, or sand. Very rich soils with high levels of organic material tend to make vines with excessive foliage, or bearing a heavy crop of late-ripening, low-sugar fruit. Leaner soils are more desirable as they give comparatively modest crops of fruit that mature earlier and have considerable sugar in the berry.

Have your soil tested *for grape growing.* A complete soil test will tell you the pH level, levels of mineral and trace elements, and make the necessary recommendations for soil improvement. If you are thinking of growing grapes commercially, you must have a complete fertilizer analysis. Often soils are not only deficient in nitrogen, phosphorus and potash (the familiar NPK), but must have small amounts of boron, magnesium, calcium and zinc added to produce grapes of good quality. It is estimated that in New England it may take as much as between 500 and 750 pounds of NPK *per acre per year* to produce four to six tons of quality grapes and the next year's new wood.

Preparing the Vineyard for the Vine

Grapes do not tolerate weeds or competitive grass. Therefore, land intended for a vineyard is usually plowed, disced, and planted to some row crop the year before the vines are set out. This reduces the number of weeds substantially.

The vineyard should be plowed deeply and should be very well disced, so that the soil is thoroughly pulverized before the vines are set out. Since grapes are usually grown on a slope in "clean cultivation" (no plant competitors allowed nearby, the vine set in bare soil), *the risk of erosion is considerable*. If your slope is more steep than gentle, your local soil conservation service specialist can help you plan the most advantageous contour rows for your vines. Good topsoil is eroding in this country at a frightening rate, and every care must be taken to prevent erosion.

Building a Trellis

Grapes require some system to support their eager vines. While grapes can be grown ornamentally along fences, for best harvest results, the vine should be trained to grow on a trellis system designed for ease of pruning and maximum sunlight. An overgrown, dense vine will not receive enough sunlight to ripen the fruit.

The trellis should be built for sturdiness and longevity. It is particularly important that the posts which support the trellis wires be strong and well-set. The end posts must be the strongest; they should be heavy and well-braced, set three feet deep and angled outward so they will not be pulled over by the weight of the mature vines. In each row the end posts should be positioned four feet from the last plants in the row. Every two or three vines, set in the line posts to carry the trellis. Remember that the posts must support the weight of the heavy foliage and fruit, and during windstorms the stresses can be powerful.

Grapevines should never be set right up against a post, for the plants will outlast any wooden post, and the roots will be disturbed when the post has to be replaced. Moreover, many wooden posts are treated with preservatives that can harm the vine. Long-lasting wooden posts are made of black locust, white oak, red cedar, and osage orange. Posts made of other wood may be treated with creosote to make them last longer.

Better than wooden posts, but quite expensive, are steel or concrete posts. But, steel posts also act as lightning rods in a vineyard on an exposed hill. Lightning has been known to run along the trellis wires and destroy a row of fruiting arms. Grape-growers who live near granite or other stone quarries may be able to get their hands on stone posts that are beautiful and last forever.

Once the posts are set, putting up the trellis wire is not unlike putting up a fence. The standard trellis consists of two or more strands of no. 9 wire stapled to cross arms on each post. The staples are not driven snug, but allow the wires to slide back and forth beneath them, so that the wires may be tightened at the end of the row with a turnbuckle when the weight of the vines causes them to sag.

Planting the Vines

Grapes should be planted as early in the spring as the soil can be worked north of Arkansas, Tennessee, and Virginia. Farther south the vines can be planted in the autumn. It is important that the plants make themselves at home and get established before the long hot days of summer begin.

Order your grape stock from a nursery as nearby as possible; if you can, pick out and pick up the plants yourself. Slow delivery and delays in transit are unfortunately the rule rather than the exception with mail-order stock; vines often arrive late, dried out, and weakened. The best stock is strong, sturdy, one-year-old plants with large fibrous root systems; two-year-old plants are more expensive, and they will not bear any sooner.

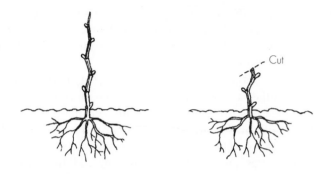

Plant the vine at the same depth it grew in the nursery. Prune it back to a single stem or three buds tall.

Dig a good hole in the worked-up soil, large enough to spread out the vine's roots comfortably. Never stuff a grapevine into a cramped miserly hole. Pack the soil firmly around the roots, leaving no air spaces that can increase the chances of disease. Plant the vines at the same depth they grew in the nursery, then prune them back to a single stem two or three buds tall. If it is early spring and the soil is moist, you need not water at planting. Later in the spring you may want to water well after planting. Watering helps the soil close in around the roots.

Space most hybrid cultivars eight to ten feet apart in the row, with the rows ten to eleven feet from each other. Less vigorous vines, like Delaware, can be closer together — seven or eight feet apart in the row.

Caring for Your Vineyard

Cultivation and Soil Management

Cultivation seems to stimulate tired vines like a Swedish massage revives an exhausted executive. Grapevines thrive with shallow cultivation, no deeper than three or four inches lest the roots be damaged, at least several times in the spring and early summer. A rototiller is very useful for this chore, but there are vine growers who cherish the hours in their vineyard with a grape hoe, one of mankind's better inventions. A session with the grape hoe will leave very few weeds behind for hand pulling.

If your vines are planted on a steep hillside, practice "trashy cultivation" to control soil erosion. Trashy cultivation means leaving some herbiage growing and some rough pockets and hillocks of soil to hold water in tiny pools rather than allowing it to run off a smooth surface and carry precious topsoil with it. It is better not to be scrupulously clean in cultivating, but to cultivate just enough to keep the weeds down and the vines up. There is always another year for the vines, but when the soil is gone — it is gone forever.

Weak vines usually perk up with cultivation. Sometimes vines that are doing poorly need only a shot of nitrogenous fertilizer, sometimes a complete fertilizer. Work organic material into the soil — rotted manure, old hay and straw, and grape pomace — all build the soil and give the vine considerable amounts of plant nutrients. If you are not sure what fertilizers you need, see your county agent and have the soil tested for grape growing conditions.

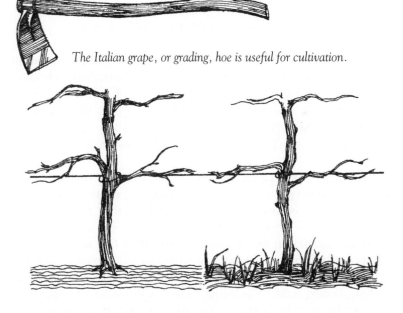

The Italian grape, or grading, hoe is useful for cultivation.

With smooth cultivation (left), as you might do in your vegetable garden, all weeds are removed and the soil is left smooth. Trashy cultivation (right) leaves rough pockets of soil and a few weeds; it is recommended to prevent soil erosion.

Sometimes the soil is so rich that the vines grow too lustily. These excessively vigorous plants may blossom heavily but set fruit sparsely and with reluctance. Grape gardeners have learned that sowing a rapid-growing cover crop such as rye or oats will take some of the nutrients away form the too-vigorous vines, restrict their growth, and force them to set their fruit. Normal cultivation should follow after the fruit sets. The same ploy worked just before the grapes ripen often makes better quality fruit and helps next year's bearing wood mature more thoroughly.

Training

Training is the business of shaping young vines into a particular system of growth by judicious pruning. There are scores of these systems, such as the Four Arm Kniffen, the Umbrella Kniffen, the Geneva Double Curtain, the Munson, the Keuka High Renewal, and many more. The Single Stem Four Cane Kniffen System is the most popular in the eastern United States and suits most bunch grapes well. However, the Geneva Double Curtain System was especially developed for vigorous cultivars like Catawba, Niagara, and that old favorite, Concord. Both the Kniffen and the Geneva Double Curtain are briefly described here. If you wish more information on training systems, consult USDA Farmers' Bulletin Number 2123, "Growing American Bunch Grapes" by grape authority J. R. McGrow. "The Geneva Double Curtain System for Vigorous Grape Vines" is available from the New York Agricultural Experiment Station at Cornell University.

The Four Arm Kniffen System (for moderately vigorous vines). For this system two wires are strung across the posts, as illustrated. The lower wire is strung about 30 inches from the ground. The top wire is run 24 inches to 30 inches above the lower wire.

Begin training in the autumn of your vine's first session, after it has become dormant. Choose the strongest looking cane and tie it with binder twine to the top wire. (Do not use wire, plastic twine, or long-lasting cord to tie grapes; these will last so long they may strangle the growing vine.) Nip off the cane just above the top wire, then cut off *all* the other canes. If the vine did not grow any canes long enough to reach the top wire, don't worry, the plant is build-

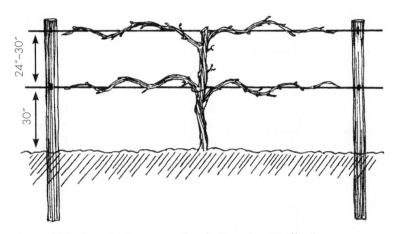

This established vine has been trained to the Four Arm Kniffen System.

ing up its root system. Simply tie the strongest cane it made to the bottom wire and nip off the other growth as above. If the vine was laggard and you do not have a cane that will reach even the bottom wire, cut the cane right back to a single stem with two or three buds as you did after the initial planting, and wait until next year. Patience is only one of the grape-grower's virtues.

In the dormant period following the second or third growing season, choose four of the strongest canes for the *arms*. Count off about ten buds along the length of each arm, and prune off all other growth, except for *renewal spurs*. Tie each arm along its horizontal wire. Near each arm's source, leave an auxiliary arm two or three buds long for renewal spurs. Every year in the dormant season the arms will be replaced by the renewal spur canes, and new sets of renewal spurs will be started. In that way, each vine will have new arms every year.

Northern gardeners with their short growing seasons will find that extending the Kniffen System trellis a foot higher so that there is more space between the wires lets greater amounts of sunlight strike the vines, and this extra sunshine can make the difference between harvest baskets full of ripe grapes or a row of frost-blasted immature bunches.

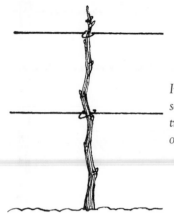

In the autumn of the vine's first season, select the strongest cane to become the trunk, tie it to the top wire, and cut off all other canes.

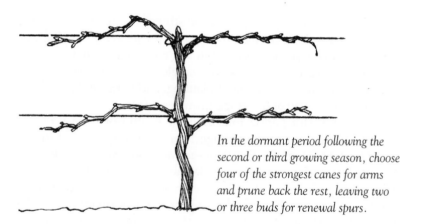

In the dormant period following the second or third growing season, choose four of the strongest canes for arms and prune back the rest, leaving two or three buds for renewal spurs.

The Geneva Double Curtain System (for vigorous vines). This system is designed to get greater amounts of sunlight on the vines, making more and better fruit.

Three wires are used in this system; the center trunk support wire is set 52 inches from the ground, and the two cordon wires support the arms. A vine can be trained so that its arms extend 16 feet along the wires.

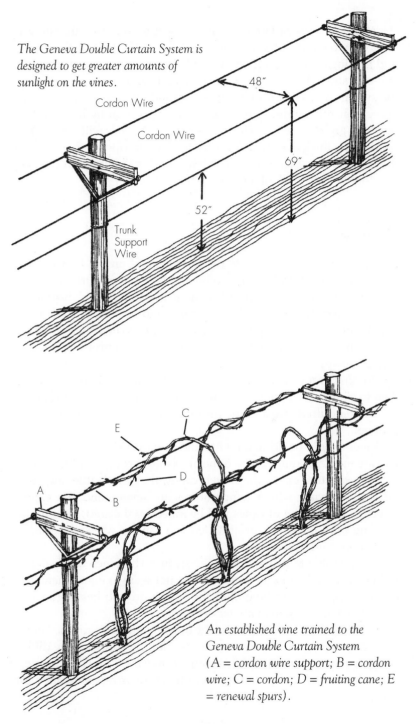

The Geneva Double Curtain System is designed to get greater amounts of sunlight on the vines.

Cordon Wire

Cordon Wire

48″

69″

52″

Trunk Support Wire

An established vine trained to the Geneva Double Curtain System (A = cordon wire support; B = cordon wire; C = cordon; D = fruiting cane; E = renewal spurs).

With the Geneva Double Curtain each vine is usually allowed to have two trunks of a more efficient use of the trellis space. Five-bud fruiting canes are left on the cordons, and the renewal spurs are one-bud stubs. If the canes were allowed to grow at their own will, the system would turn into a mass of random greenery. However, every year the fruiting canes are tied into position by hand so that they will grow *downward*. The leaves receive the sun; with grapes it is sunlight on the leaves which causes the fruit to ripen rather than on the fruit clusters themselves. The effect of this system in midseason is a double curtain of foliage, hence the name.

Pruning

Once the young vines are porperly shaped on the trellis to the system you want and begin producing, they are mature vines and must be maintained by heavy annual pruning. Many beginning grape gardeners are timid about pruning and hesitate to slash away healthy growth. But grape growers must learn to be ruthless, for the vines cannot give a decent crop without thorough pruning. There is a limit, however; too much pruning will discourage the vines.

Pruning grapevines is a fairly simple operation. There are no ladders to climb, no "wrong" cutting angles to worry about, no special tools are required. Most grape pruning jobs can be done with hand pruners.

Vines should be dormant when they are pruned. Where the winters are mild, pruning can be done at leisure throughout the winter. But never prune or handle frozen canes; they are brittle and snap off easily. If your winter temperatures are severe, and you expect a certain percentage of canes will be killed by the cold, hold off on pruning until the early spring when you can see which canes have made it through the winter.

It is possible to prune late in the spring. The vines will leak sap rather alarmingly, but the practice does not seem to injure them. But late pruning and handling after the spring growth has begun will almost certainly injure many tender buds.

How much to cut off? This is the burning question for the beginning grape-grower. The answer varies with the cultivar. The different grape varieties are divided into "long cane," "medium cane," and "short cane" vines, and different handling is recommended for each.

- *Long cane:* These vines should keep between thirty and sixty buds on each plant after they are pruned. Serious vine growers weigh the pruned wood on a balance scale. They leave a basic thirty buds on the vine, plus ten more buds for each pound of year-old wood pruned out.
- *Medium cane:* Leave twenty-five basic buds plus an additional ten for each pound of wood pruned out.
- *Short cane:* These cultivars bear large clusters of grapes and should be severely nipped back. For the first pound of cuttings taken off, only four to six buds are allowed to remain. A scant two buds are granted for each additional pound of wood removed.

Just as artists begin a painting by "roughing out" a sketch, experienced pruners begin by roughing out the whole vine to conform to its particular training system. They leave plenty of extra buds as a margin, weigh the cuttings, then "fine prune" the vine to its proper balance. After a few seasons the eye and the hand are all that's necessary to tell how much to take off.

Long Cane	Medium Cane	Short Cane
Beta	Blue Lake	Seibel 9110 (Verdelet)
Caco	Catawba	Seyve-Villard 5-276 (Seyval Blanc)
Campbell Early	Concord Seedless	
Concord	Delaware	Seyve-Villard 12-375 (Villard Blanc)
Fredonia	Ellen Scott	
Foch	Golden Muscat	Seyve-Villard 18-315 (Villard Noir)
Niagara	Himrod	
Worden	Interlaken Seedless	
	Landot 244 (Landal)	
	Moore Early	
	Seibel 5279 (Aurore)	
	Seibel 13053 (Cascade)	
	Seneca	
	Steuben	
	Stover	
	Vidal 256	

New Trunks for Old. It is not unusual for vine trunks to grow feeble through disease or damage and falter after some years. It is faster, takes less work, and means less crop loss to develop a new trunk than to take out the whole vine and start over.

To renew a trunk, allow a healthy sucker from the base of the damaged trunk to develop. Train it up the trellis just as though it were a young vine.

At the end of two seasons the basic form of the new trunk and its arms will be established. Start decreasing the canes on the old trunk system so that the new trunk can gather the strength to put out a crop. At the end of the third season, cut out the old trunk altogether during the dormant period.

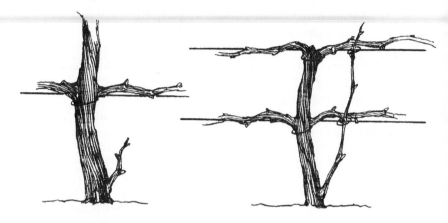

To replace a feeble trunk, allow a healthy sucker to develop (left) and train it up the trellis like a young vine (right).

The Killing Spring Frost. Northern gardeners and grape growers learn to develop a sixth sense for weather changes that mean a late frost and are usually able to protect their plants from the damaging ice crystal formations. But sometimes the worst happens, and the tender new growth on the vines is badly damaged by a killer frost. If the damage is severe, you can still get a partial crop by *stripping* the new growth to force secondary buds to develop. If the frost damage is light and has just hit the tips, do *not* strip. You still may get only a partial crop through incomplete fruit set, but that's all you'd get with stripping, too.

Stripping is something of a last resort, the difference between some grapes and no grapes. With your hands or a pair of hand pruners completely strip the vines of *all* new growth, both the frosted and the unfrosted shoots. (Partial stripping is not good; it leads to mal-formed vines that will be difficult to prune in following years.) The stripped vine will be forced to develop secondary buds, which will flower and fruit and give you a partial crop.

Propagation

Bunch grapes usually grow on their own roots and do not have to be grafted onto special rootstocks. They are easily propagated from cuttings taken from the previous season's growth, a simple procedure with good and economical results.

Cuttings should be taken fairly early in the dormant season to avoid the possibility of getting winter-damaged wood. Select ma-tured canes at least one-third inch in diameter. Avoid spindly or thick canes.

From vigorous cultivars like Beta or Concord, take canes with the buds three to five inches apart, and be sure there are at least three buds on the section you cut. From less vigorous vines, such as Delaware, choose canes that have the buds closer together, and cut four-bud sections.

Mallet cuttings include a small heel of two-year-old wood, and are more apt to root strongly than the one-year growth.

Bundle the cuttings with the buds pointing in the same direction and store them over the winter to plant in early spring if you live in the north. Southern grape-growers can set out cuttings in the grape nursery any time during the dormant season. The cuttings can be kept over the winter by burying them in well-drained soil covered with heavy mulch, or by packing them in moist sand or sawdust and storing in an unheated cellar. A small amount of cuttings can be kept in the refrigerator in plastic bags if they are packed in moist peat moss or sawdust.

In the early spring set out the cuttings in prepared soil that is weed-free, fertile, and in good tilth. The rows should be two to four feet apart, and the plants set four to six inches apart within the row. Set the cuttings firmly with one bud above the soil. Keep the nursery bed weed-free through the growing season. The following spring the yearling plants are ready to go into the vineyard.

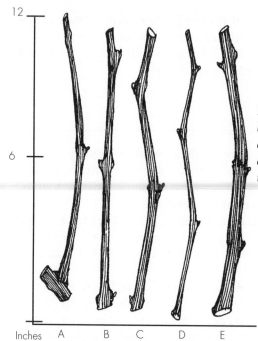

12 —

6 —

Inches   A   B   C   D   E

Bunch grapes can be propagated by cuttings. Cutting A is a mallet cutting; B and C are good cane cuttings; D is too thin; and E is too thick.

Grafting. Special rootstocks to improve the vigor of weak cultivars, or that are resistant to phylloxera or nematode infestations of the soil, or that hasten or delay wood maturity, or are adapted to dry and alkaline soils are available. Scions from the desired varieties may be grafted or chip-budded onto these stocks, but since not all stocks and scions are compatible, it is best to check with your nursery, county agent, or state extension service for information on the rootstocks that suit your special problems and the best grafting techniques.

Layering. Layering is a good propagation technique when you need to fill a vacancy left by a deceased vine in the vineyard. A young plant fresh from the nursery may have trouble competing with mature vineyard neighbors, but a layered vine will usually do very well.

Layering is best done in spring. Choose a sturdy cane on a vine neighbor near the vacancy. At the place you want the new vine to grow, dig a shallow trench three or four inches deep and fill it halfway with rich, well-worked soil. Bend down the chosen cane so it lies in the trench with two buds protruding above the surface, and two or three buds lie below the soil. Pack the soil down firmly. You may have to put a brick on it to hold the cane down. Let the cane tip grow freely through the summer. In the autumn dormant period the connection with the parent plant can be severed if the new vine has done well. Otherwise, let it develop a strong root system through another season.

Diseases and Pests of the Grape

Humans are not alone in loving grapes; the sugar-rich berries and succulent vines and roots are banquet material for hundreds of insect species. Few birds can resist a vine of ripe grapes. Indeed, eighty-four species of birds feast on grapes, as do black bears, coyotes, foxes, possums, raccoons, skunks, and squirrels. White-tailed deer enthusiastically nibble foliage and canes. Nets, fences, alarms, scarecrows, flapping and noise-making objects, deterrent scents, and many other items are sold each year to grape-growers anxious to protect the fruits of their labor.

A few of the grape-damaging insects are: *Japanese beetles*; *curculio*; *cutworms* that gnaw the buds at night; *thrips* that suck the plant's vital juices; *rose chafers* that devour buds, blossoms, new fruits, and leaves; the larvae of *grape moths* that devour the pulp of the berries; *flea beetles*, partial to the vine and its leaves; and the infamous *phylloxera*, a sucking louse which destroyed the pure viniferous vineyards of Europe in the nineteenth century.

Organic gardeners find grapes one of the most difficult crops to grow well without sprays. Still, there are those who claim good results by keeping a well-situated vineyard isolated, scrupulously clean, and by encouraging birdlife in the vineyard, at least until the fruit begins to ripen. Knocking the insects off the vine with a jet of water from the garden hose is a deterrent, as are the practices of sprinkling soot, lime, or ashes on the leaves in the morning when the dew is still on the plants. The more visible creatures such as slugs, chafers, and Japanese beetles can be hand-picked off the vines and drowned. Some gardeners find placing a jar of decomposing rose chafers under the vine makes a nasty odor that sends survivor chafers away. Since rose chafer larvae must feed on grass roots, clean cultivation will keep these pests at bay.

In their natural state, grapes grow high in the tops of trees where they are well-ventilated. Wild grapes are hardy, bothered by few insects or diseases. Man has brought the domestic grape down to his level and pays for the convenience of its artificial posture by watching numerous fungus diseases attack the vines in damp, ill-ventilated, shaded, crowded conditions. *Bird's eye rot*, or *anthracnose*, spots the fruit, leaves, and new sprouts; *black rot* shrivels the berries; *dead arm* eventually moves from the arms to the main trunk and kills the vine; *downy mildew*, a fuzzy grey fungus killer is a bad problem with *Vitis vinifera* and hybrids in eastern vineyards.

Sprays. There are many different fungicides and insecticides on the market for combating grape pests. Commercial growers are forced by economic necessity to depend on a heavy spray schedule to make a profitable crop. Home growers can experiment with organic methods and light, but regular, applications of botanical sprays such as hellebore and pyrethrum, if they are willing to take less than full crops and accept blemished fruit.

Consistent quality and quantity grapes may be possible only by following a scheduled chemical spray program. Many home grape-growers will be able to get away with only three sprays a season, but in vineyards where disease or insects have a stranglehold on the vines, and if there is a long run of wet weather, as many as ten or twelve spray applications may be necessary.

Because spray programs must be tailored to suit the particular vineyard with its own special problems, no cut-and-dried schedule can be applied equally to all. Growers have to recognize the particular pests or diseases that menace their grapes and select and apply the proper spray at the right time. Your county agent is the first one to consult. A helpful guide is Farmers' Bulletin Number 1893, "Control of Grape Diseases and Insects in the Eastern United States," free from the Office of Communication, U.S. Department of Agriculture, Washington, D.C. 20250.

Since new pesticides (and new restrictions on old pesticides) are constantly appearing, always check with the county agent or nearest cooperative extension service for the latest recommendations on effective, safe pesticides.

Harvest

Granted healthy, pruned, well-nourished plants; good cultivation; plenty of sunshine — and a bit of luck — you will find yourself the possessor of heavy clusters of gloriously fragrant blue, purple, red, or golden grapes at harvest time. But are they really ripe? Color is a poor indicator of grape ripeness. Some people judge by taste. Others look at the seeds: green seeds mean unripe grapes, brown seeds show maturity. A change in stem color from green to brown is another index to ripeness. Winemakers, who need completely ripe grapes with high sugar levels, will test a little of the fresh juice with a hydrometer.

Although the difference in quality between ripe and unripe grapes is considerable, northern gardeners may be forced to pick early by the threat of impending frost. Unfortunately, grapes do not continue to ripen after they are picked.

Bird damage just before complete ripeness is a problem everywhere; netting, available from nurseries and garden suppliers, is a good investment. If you are a bird fancier you can always leave one or two vines uncovered, as a reward to the birds who picked insects off your vines earlier in the season.

If you have only a few vines, or if you cannot locate any netting, you might want to bag your clusters of grapes with small, white paper bags well on in the season. Brown paper bags give the fruit a disagreeable baggy flavor like a damp grocery sack. Do not use plastic bags. Bagging keeps grapes safe from birds and early frosts. Cut the bottom corner off the bags to let rain water drain out rapidly.

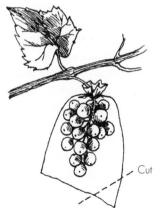

Protect your grapes from birds by bagging your clusters. Be sure to cut off a bottom corner to allow rain to drain.

When you harvest, always snip off the clusters of fruit with a pair of grape or pruning shears; "picking" grapes is not easy, for the wood is tough and you usually end up with mangled and torn stems, squashed grapes, and a bad temper.

Enjoying the Harvest

Wine is the outstanding product of the grape; but grapes also have a place of honor in the kitchen and on the table. Although grape lovers claim the best way to enjoy a ripe, fragrant cluster of delicious grapes is to eat them out of hand in the sunny vineyard, grapes make excellent pies, jams, jellies, juices, compotes, and conserves.

Grape Cultivars

Plant your vineyard with grape cultivars selected for their suitability to your climate. (R = red; B=blue; R–B = red to blue; W = white or green)

Early Cultivars

Beta (B): An extremely hardy, vigorous, and productive grape. The small berries have a wild flavor, high sugar and high acid content. Makes excellent juice and jelly.

Blue Jay (B): A cold, hardy, early grape used for juice, jelly, and the table when thoroughly ripe. Unlike most grapes listed here, it needs cross-pollination.

Edelweiss (W): This vine, like the Swenson Red, comes from Minnesota. It is very hardy, and makes a decent white wine that is below average in sugar. It grows where few other grapes can.

Foch (Kuhlmann 188-2) (B): A very early grape, but only moderately productive. It has small berries in tight little bunches. It is a very popular grape with winemakers, making a Burgundy-type wine. Birds love it, so nets are needed.

Himrod (W): Hardier than Interlaken Seedless but ripens a few days later. Large, loose clusters of sweet yellow grapes that are almost seedless make it a superior table grape and a popular roadside-market fruit.

Interlaken Seedless (W): Only moderately vigorous and productive, somewhat tender to cold, and often needs a careful spray program. A delicious and popular eating grape, almost seedless. A good roadside-market seller.

Red Amber (R): Another of the very hardy vines which produce sweet, medium-sized table fruit.

Seibel 5297 (Aurore) (W): Very early, vigorous, extremely hardy, and very productive, this fine vine gives pinkish grapes in medium-long loose clusters. The fruit is delicious to eat and makes an excellent, delicate white wine.

Seibel 13053 (Cascade) (B): Very early, vigorous, moderately hardy, and productive, this vine makes a superior rosé wine and a good blending wine for Foch.

Seneca (W): Productive, moderately vigorous, and hardy. Gives medium-sized clusters of superb, crisp berries of outstanding table quality with a sweet, winy flavor. Often named the outstanding white dessert grape. Powdery mildew is often a problem.

Swenson Red (R): A very hardy, early, vigorous vine, the juice has a good acid-to-sugar ratio and is used to make white and rosé wines. This cultivar, along with Beta and Edelweiss, can take temperatures of 30°F below zero and colder without root, trunk, or arm damage or complete winterkill. All three are prizes for the northern grape-grower.

Van Buren (B): A vigorous, productive, very early Concord-type grape. Its succulent flesh makes it a favorite with northern growers who cannot grow Concord.

Midseason Cultivars

Caco (R): A vigorous, moderately productive, and hardy vine whose large fruits are attractive if not particularly outstanding. A table fruit and roadside-market grape.

Catawba (R–B): Vigorous, productive, and hardy with large clusters of big grapes. A commercial grower's favorite for wine, juice, and table.

Concord (B): The leading commercial grape in North America with the familiar foxy flavor. It is vigorous, productive, hardy, but needs at least 170 frost-free days to ripen properly. It is used for juice, jelly, and specialty wines. This seedless cultivar is a favorite with pie fanciers.

Fredonia (B): This vigorous, productive, and hardy vine gives large berries with a mild Concord-like flavor. A sort of Fredonia, McCampbell, is an excellent roadside-stand seller with its large clusters of big, bursting berries.

Golden Muscat (W): This fine, golden-yellow grape is vigorous, moderately productive, and hardy. It likes a somewhat cool summer with plenty of sun to ripen properly. A table grape with a mild, foxy taste.

Landot 244 (Landal) (B): Moderate vigor and production. Fully ripened fruit makes good wine.

Moore Early (B): This is hardy, but only moderately vigorous and with poor productivity. Its charm lies in its being a Concord type that ripens about two weeks earlier than Concord, though the fruit often cracks.

Niagara (W): A foxy-flavored, large-berried fruit. The vine is hardy, vigorous, and productive. Good table fruits.

Seibel 9110 (Verdelet) (W): Vigorous, but not a steady producer. Apt to be sensitive to cold. The grapes are a beautiful yellow-gold, an excellent dessert grape which also makes good wine.

Seyve-Villard 5-276 (Seyval Blanc) (W): A medium vigorous vine with good disease resistance, largely grown for the superior quality white wine it makes.

Steuben (B): Vigorous, productive, somewhat hardy and disease resistant, Steuben is an increasingly popular commercial grape. The sweet grapes in their long, tapering clusters have an unusual spicy flavor.

Worden (B): Hardy, productive, and vigorous, the vine gives large Concord-type grapes of equal quality with Concord. Fruit sometimes cracks. Good juice and jelly grape, ripening about ten days earlier than Concord.

Late-Season Cultivars

Delaware (R): Hardy, but medium to low vigor and production. The small grapes ripen from pink to deep mahogany with a high sugar content. These are table grapes of considerable popularity.

Ellen Scott (R): A vigorous and productive vine that is not very hardy. Susceptible to disease. It is usually grown as a table and juice grape in the South. The fruit is large and juicy.

SeyveVillard 12-375 (Villard Blanc) (W): Vigorous, very productive, highly disease resistant. A regular producer of large, loose clusters of grapes widely planted for wine and used also for dessert grapes.

Seyve-Villard 18-315 (Villard Noir) (B): This is a standard grape in southern France, a late red of low vigor but quite hardy. It makes a sound but ordinary good red wine — *un vin ordinaire*.

Vidal 256 (W): A very vigorous, hardy, heavy producer. It is grown for wine, which has a good aroma and is neutral, clean, rated good to very good. If hit by spring frost damage, it can still produce a moderate secondary crop.

Gulf Coast and Florida Cultivars

Blue Lake (B–R): The vine produces in early midseason and gives the grower clusters of small grapes with a unique aromatic spiciness. The fruit is poor for shipping or storing; it is usually made into juice and jelly.

Stover (W): This special vine must be grafted and is then moderately vigorous, productive, hardy, and resistant to Pierce's Disease. It must be sprayed for foliage diseases. Produces white table fruit of quality superior to Blue Lake.

Wine Grapes for East Coast Growers

The New York State Fruit Testing Cooperative Association (NYSFTCA) lists the following *Vitis vinifera* cultivars. (West Coast growers will have little trouble locating a source of *Vitis vinifera* stock through county agents and extension service recommendations.)

Cabernet Sauvignon (R): A variety that gained its fame through the red wines of Bordeaux. An outstanding grape for the finest Médoc clarets, it rarely ripens well enough at Geneva to make a notable wine.

Chardonnay (W): One of the more hardy *vinefera* cultivars, this is the grape that makes white burgundies.

Gamay (R): This grape makes red wine and is temperamental. Grown in Burgundy its wine is ordinary; in Beaujolais, it is superb. In California plantings, the wine from the mountain vineyards in Santa Cruz are markedly superior to the Gamay wine of the Napa Valley. It is a late ripener. The NYSFTCA notes that it is more productive than the other *V. vinifera* they list.

Gewürztraminer (W): The spiciest flavored wine grapes and the basis of many delicious Alsatian and German fruity wines. Less hardy with the Geneva, NY, climate than White Riesling and Chardonnay, it has produced excellent wines there.

Pinot Noir (R): One of the greatest and most famous fine wine grapes, this is the source of the great red Burgundies and Champagne. The vine is infamous for being "difficult." At Geneva it has made the best red wines of their collection, but not of a quality to compare with the wine it makes in France. The Geneva-made wine was notably lacking in color and body.

White Riesling (W): The source of the noble wines of Alsace, the Moselle and the Rhine, White Riesling is one of the great grapes of the wine world. It is grown not only in Europe, but in Chile and California, and it makes a flowery, aromatic wine. At Geneva this variety has made outstanding white wines and appears to be, with Chardonnay, the most promising *Vitis vinifera* for growing in the north.

Cold Hardiness

The University of New Hampshire Cooperative Extension Service Bulletin, "Cultural Techniques for Growing Grapes in New Hampshire," is concerned not only with early ripening dates, but with *cold hardiness* of grape cultivars. Here is how they rank some popular hybrid bunch grapes.

Most Hardy			Hardy	Medium Hardy	Low in Hardiness
1	2	3	4	5	6
Beta	Clinton	Concord	Niagara	Baco 1	White Riesling
Blue Jay	Brighton	Fredonia	Delaware	Portland	Interlaken Seedless
Red Amber		Worden	Van Buren	Steuben	Romulus
		Seibel 1000	Buffalo	Other hybrids	
			Foch	Golden Muscat	
			Agawan		
			Other hybrids		

Information for Grape-Growers

Sources for Grape Vines

Gurney's Seed & Nursery Co.
513-354-1491
www.gurneys.com

Indiana Berry & Plant Co.
800-295-2226
http://indianaberry.com

Inter-State Nurseries
309-663-6797
www.interstatenurseries.com

Miller Nurseries
800-836-9630
www.millernurseries.com

Stark Bro's Nurseries & Orchards Co.
800-325-4180
www.starkbros.com

More Information

The USDA and the State Agricultural Experiment Stations issue leaflets and bulletins that cover recommended cultivars, growing techniques, identification of diseases and pests of grapes, and spray programs to combat specific problems. States such as California, Washington, Oregon, and New York, where there are extensive commercial grape plantings and associated grape industries, offer considerably more information. Consult your local extension agent. Canadian grape growers should contact the Department of Plant Agriculture at the University of Guelph in Ontario (*www.oac.uoguelph.ca*) and the Central Experimental Farm in Ottawa (613-759-1837).

Many publications are now out of print, but often are still available online. One place to check is the list on the Web site of the New York State Agricultural Experiment Station at *www. nysaes.cornell.edu/hp/publications.html*.

Other Storey Titles You Will Enjoy

Cellaring Wine, by Jeff Cox.
A sourcebook to create a system for selecting wines to age, storing them properly, and drinking them when they are just right.
272 pages. Paper. ISBN 978-1-58017-474-9.

From Vines to Wines, by Jeff Cox.
A complete home winemaking education
in one book — from planting vines to pulling the cork.
256 pages. Paper. ISBN 978-1-58017-105-2.

The Gardener's A–Z Guide to Growing Organic Food,
by Tanya L. K. Denckla.
An invaluable resource for growing, harvesting, and storing 765 varieties of vegetables, fruits, herbs, and nuts.
496 pages. Paper. ISBN 978-1-58017-370-4.

The Home Winemaker's Companion,
by Gene Spaziani and Ed Halloran.
A guide for all levels, starting with your first batch of kit wine to mastering advanced techniques for making wine from fresh grapes.
272 pages. Paper. ISBN 978-1-58017-209-7.

Landscaping with Fruit, by Lee Reich.
A complete, accessible guide to luscious landscaping — from alpine strawberry to lingonberry, mulberry to wintergreen.
192 pages. Paper. ISBN 978-1-60342-091-4.
Hardcover with jacket. ISBN 978-1-60342-096-9.

The Winemaker's Answer Book, by Alison Crowe.
A reassuring reference that offers proven solutions to every wine-making mishap, written by *WineMaker* magazine's Wine Wizard.
384 pages. Flexibind. ISBN 978-1-58017-656-9.

These and other books from Storey Publishing are available wherever quality books are sold or by calling 1-800-441-5700.
Visit us at *www.storey.com.*